Life with Bee

A Faith-Based Growth Mindset Journal

Grades 3rd - 7th

Written and Illustrated by
Jena' Lowry

Published by Kainon Land Media
Pace, Florida
www.kainonlandmedia.com
www.jenalowry.com
Printed in the United States of America

ISBN: 979-8-9870072-1-1
Title: Life with Bee:
        A Faith-Based Growth Mindset Journal
        for Grades 3rd - 7th

Scripture quotations are from the (KJV), King James Version, the (NKJV), New King James Version, the (ISV), International Standard Version, and the (NHEB), New Heart English Bible.

Written and Illustrated by Jena' Lowry

Contributors:
Bre' Lowry, Katie Cook, and Ainsley Cook

Dedicated to
Kathleen Meredith Joiner
Who taught me the love of God,
and who walked daily, in the
Fruit of The Spirit.
We will always remember and
we'll always be grateful.
-Love, your children and grandchildren

Meet our Contributors!

Bre' Lowry

Bre', whose nickname is Bee, enjoys collaborating with her adoptive mom, Jena'. Together, they have created the Life with Bee children's book series. Bre' and her mom understand the need for representation of multiracial characters, and children of Faith.
Fun Fact: On each cover of Life with Bee a "blue ribboned heart" can be seen on the character's shirt, in recognition of Child Abuse Awareness.

Katie Cook:

Katie is a Dual-Certified Teacher. She has a Bachelor of Arts in Elementary Education, K-6, and Elementary Special Education K-12. Katie specializes in working with Neurodiverse Students in a Social-Thinking classroom setting to assist students in developing social-emotional regulation skills.

Ainsley Cook:

Ainsley and her mom, Katie, creatively use their skills to develop educational materials that children will find both engaging and fun. Ainsley is an avid reader, and understands the joy of offering books and resources that students will enjoy!

This Journal belongs to

____

My Growth Mindset Journal

Hi everyone!

Thank you for adding this journal to your reading.

I'm excited for you! Remember that choosing to

walk in the "Fruit of The Spirit" isn't always easy,

but it is always REWARDING!

I'm glad I made the choice!

When we learn, then we grow, and that's an

AWESOME THING!

I hope you enjoy these activities, and will

complete the entire journal. If you miss a day

or two, no worries, just come back to it as

soon as you can! Be committed to finishing it...

you won't be disappointed!

Talk soon,

Your friend Bee

See this broken shell?
Even broken things are beautiful...
it's a choice in how we see it...
It's called "perspective!"

Why...
do I need this journal?

I'm so glad you asked  To GROW!

No, not like physically growing on the outside, but growing on the INSIDE! We need to make sure we're learning things like how to "think healthy", btw, if you haven't read Life with Bee, the Crazy Cool Glove, you need to!

Are you ready?
Me too!
Go ahead... turn the page

So, my family and I were talking about the importance
of doing things, to keep our minds and hearts "ready"…
It's sorta like the military, or police officers.
They learn & practice drills/skills
to make sure they're ready before the attack,
or before they face stressful situations.
We're kinda that way too.
We should think of ways to keep our minds, and hearts
SAFE… before we're in difficult situations!

One skill to practice is
"catching thoughts" like these,
BEFORE they cause PROBLEMS!

Your turn... In these bubbles, write negative thoughts that you've had about yourself.
Hey, thank you for sharing your thoughts! It's important to feel safe to share things.

Negative thoughts aren't
always about ourself...
sometimes they might be
about other people...

Everyone has
THOUGHTS

The problem is, thoughts are either
HEALTHY or UNHEALTHY.
We ALL have these things called "pet peeves"
that can cause frustrating thoughts.
Our job, is to recognize when thoughts are
creating frustrating feelings.
We have to "catch them" BEFORE they
create issues! Okay, let's find out what your
"Pet Peeve" is... (turn the page)

My Growth Mindset

Do you have a "Pet Peeve?"

Draw a picture of
YOURSELF
feeling frustrated.

Remember, EVERYONE gets frustrated

Okay, so now that we
understand that EVERYONE
gets frustrated...
let's talk about the "healthy"
things we can do,
that help us
continue moving forward!

Put on your shoes, okay
actually you can be barefoot...
take a look at the "choices"
on the next page...

Things I can do 

(Circle) the phrases that help you choose Self-Control
when you're feeling frustrated

Take slow
deep breaths

Slam my door

Read my
bible & talk
to God

Yell
at someone

Find a safe
quiet place
to think and
reflect

Talk to someone
I trust

Remind myself
that I can't
change other
people

Remind myself
that God
helps me

Call someone a
bad name

Be
dishonest

Remind myself
that I CAN change
my reactions

Write POSITIVE phrases
on paper and place them
where I can read them
every day

Remind myself
that God loves me

Hey, turn to the last page...
I have something for you!
(You can hang it up)

LIST THE NINE
FRUITS OF THE SPIRIT
USING THE LINES BELOW

_______________________________   _______________________________

_______________________________   _______________________________

_______________________________   _______________________________

_______________________________   _______________________________

____

HINT:
CHECK OUT THE NEXT PAGE...

The Fruit of The Spirit

Inside of the circle, write a
Fruit of The Spirit
that is difficult for you to do.

Remember we all struggle.
It's okay if you list more than one

Love　Joy　Peace　Patience　Kindness　Goodness　Faithfulness　Gentleness　and　Self-Control

Galatians 5:22-23

Choose FRUIT instead of "cramming candy bars!"

What are some "unhealthy thoughts" I need to catch? (write them here)

My Goal this week: Work on catching unhealthy thoughts. [list the FRUITS that can help]

How can I help myself reach my GOAL

Okay it's "fess-up" time

That's what my grandma calls
(confession time)

Have you ever had someone say or
do something that was
SUPER EMBARRASSING for you?!?
How did you feel?
Did you want to become invisible?
Or did you want to get back at
them?

Think about words that are associated
with what you were feeling & thinking,
and write those words here...

Hey, make this a FRUITY PAGE!

Fill this page with fruit!

(it can be your own drawings or stickers)

kiwi

oranges

grapes

apples

lime

tangerines

watermelon

pineapple

Okay, let's review! 

So now we know the nine Fruits, right!?!

And we understand that choosing them,

can help us make healthy choices

in difficult situations.

Guess what?

God knew we would need help.

I bet when you've worked on a STEM

project or worked on a Lego build,

you needed the INSTRUCTIONS to help.

Instructions are super important!

They help ensure that what we're building

is strong and will last!

That's exactly why God gave us the Bible.

Think of it as His instructions to help us

NOT FALL APART!

Your Turn!

In this space write
INSTRUCTIONS
(step-by-step how to) for
something you enjoy doing

Here are a few examples:

*Making French-Toast

*Creating an origami animal

*Creating a paper-airplane

*Playing your favorite video-game, or board game

*Making a peanut-butter and pickle sandwich (yep, it's delicious!)

Hey, did you try making a peanut butter and pickle sandwich?
It's okay if you didn't some people have allergies to peanuts.

In this space draw a picture of the thing you gave instructions for (from the previous page).
I bet you did a great job writing the instructions!

*Challenge Time

The next two pages will help you
learn how to find things in your Bible.
That's a super important skill...
and you're going to do GREAT!

Did you know that most books have
"Table of Contents"... even BIBLES!
And you can use the one in the FRONT
of your Bible, to complete the next page,

The Bible is made up of sixty-six <u>books</u>
each book has <u>chapters</u>
and each chapter has <u>verses</u>

Ready! Here we go!
Go ahead, turn the page...

After you've found
the matching bubble,
place a check ✓ in the box

☐ Jeremiah 29:11-13

☐ Romans 8:38-39

☐ Joshua 1:9

☐ Colossians 3:12-15

Things God Teaches ME

Look at YOU
Wow!
You read all of those verses!

I'm so proud of you,
and God is too!

It's awesome to read the Bible!
Remember in the beginning, when we
talked about choosing
"healthy things" for the
INSIDE of us?
The Bible is not only filled with awesome
instructions for us, but as we read it,
we're "washing" (cleaning) our mind and
heart.
It's cleaning us on the inside!

Have you ever seen a set of GEARS?

They "connect together" so that all the parts can keep moving!

As we "connect together" with the Bible, we are connecting ourselves with God. And you know what, He is a really GOOD FRIEND to connect with!

Read the next page,
then use this page
to create!

Okay, your turn!

Think about things you connect with.
For example, your family, your church, your friends.
Maybe you're on a sports team, or in a Fine Arts
group like theater, music, photography,
or dance company.
Maybe you enjoy writing.

Inside of the GEARS
write the things
YOU connect with.

Ready for a challenge?
On the previous blank page, draw more gears!
Then add the names of people, and activities
that you are GRATEFUL to be connected to.

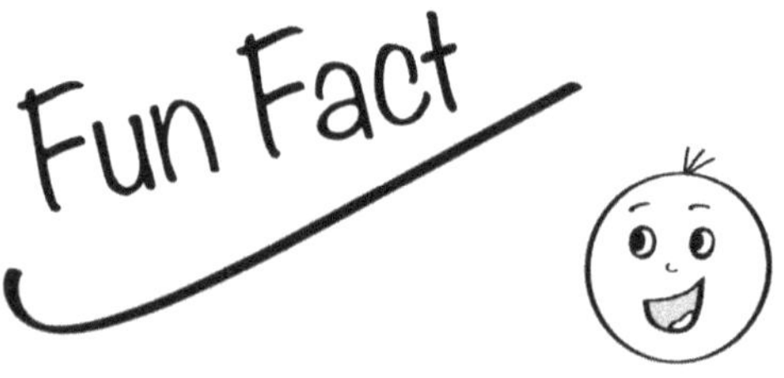

Fun Fact

My Mom and I created
Life with Bee
to help kids connect,
and understand that
"putting into practice"
the things we learn from
the Bible
really isn't hard at all!

Start here
Finish here

Sometimes things look harder than they really are. When you first looked at the maze, you probably thought, "Um, this might be a little difficult", but by the end you knew it really wasn't as hard as you thought. That's what reading your Bible is like. At first, it might seem difficult. But after you start, you'll realize it really isn't hard at all.

Pause Break

Before turning the page, let's take a moment to talk about Salvation, which means "to save".
You might ask, "Why do I need to be saved, I'm not in danger?"
Guess what? Everyone on earth entered danger when they were born.
Let's back up a minute.
You've heard of "Adam & Eve", right? They were the first people God created. They were given a rule from God... but they broke it. Then tried to hide from Him. They sinned against God. And because they sinned, it required them to be cleaned [on the inside].
Remember earlier when we said reading the Bible was like "washing" on the inside? Well, when we make a choice to believe in God, then we also except that He sent His son, JESUS as a way for us to be cleaned (forgiven) of our sin.

Take a moment to read
John, chapter 3, verses 16 and 17.
Then, Romans, chapter 10, verse 13
You'll need these for the next page!

Romans 10:13, John 3:16, John 3:17

Look up these verses above, then...

**Write the book, chapter, and verse
on the line
under the phrase it matches**

"Everyone who calls on the
name of the Lord, will be
saved"

____

"For God so loved the world that He gave His
one and only Son, that whoever believes in
Him will not perish but have eternal life"

____

"For God did not send His Son into the
world to condemn the world, but that
the world through Him might be saved

____

Isn't it AWESOME that God loves us so much
that He gave us a way to be
Forgiven.

Have you ever had a moment [or two] when you weren't very
nice to someone?
Did you tell them you were sorry?

Saying "I'm sorry" for something you did, that
hurt someone, can sometimes be challenging, but
once you apologize...
WOW! You will feel soooo much better!

Let's Practice!
In this space, write words
(or phrases) that you can
say to someone you may
have hurt

Take a quick look at Colossians, chapter 3, verses 12-15
[Colossians 3:12-15]

When you get cold do you put on a jacket?
Most of us do, because it's a way to stay warm,
and protect ourselves from the cold.

Think of God's Word the same way...
we need to put it on [wear it]
over our mind
because it keeps us protected.

{Put on} therefore, as God's chosen ones, holy and
beloved, a heart of compassion, kindness,
gentleness, humility, and patience;
bearing with one another, and forgiving each other,
if anyone has a complaint against you, just as the
Lord has forgiven you, you also should forgive.
Above all these things, walk in love, which is the
bond of perfection.
And let the peace of Christ rule in your hearts,
to which also you were called
in one body; and be thankful.
Colossians 3:12 - 15

Before we continue, can we pray together?

Awesome!
Praying is another thing
that isn't complicated. It's [us and God]
talking, just like when you talk with your
family, or your best friend.
You may want to ask a question,
you may want to say "Thank you",
or you just might want to share something
that's personal to you.
Whatever you want to say, or share,
God is a GREAT listener!

God, thank you for loving us. And thank you for hearing us,

and listening when we want to talk with you. We love you.

God, we invite You to come into our hearts, wash us clean

from our sin, and forgive us. We invite You to stay in our

hearts forever. Thank You for being our best friend.

In Jesus' name, Amen

Love Bee ___________________
write your name here

Have you ever lost something that's super VALUABLE to you?

Someone else might not have thought it was valuable... but to you, it meant everything!
You loved it, and knew how important it was to you.
After you lost it, did you search for it?
If you didn't find it right away, did you give up the search?

Guess what?!?
Before you invited Jesus into your heart, you were lost too. But Jesus kept looking for you. He didn't give up on you, because He knows how VALUABLE you are!
He LOVES you!
And now, because you invited Him to live in your heart, you are no longer LOST!

You are valuable! 

Make a list of people
who love you…

____

____

____

____

____

List the things YOU
love about yourself…

____

____

____

____

____

John 15:9
"Even as the Father has loved me, I also have
loved YOU. Remain in my love." -Jesus

Hey, let's do four more bubbles!

btw, did you know parents can download a Bible app on their cellphone for FREE!

But before you start, say this with me...
"I AM LOVED"
Gosh, doesn't that make you feel great!
Yeah, me too!
I love reminding myself that I AM LOVED!

☐ 2 Corinthians 5:17

☐ Psalm 18:32

☐ Psalm 139:14

☐ Ephesians 1:4

Don't forget to place a check in your boxes on this page and the next

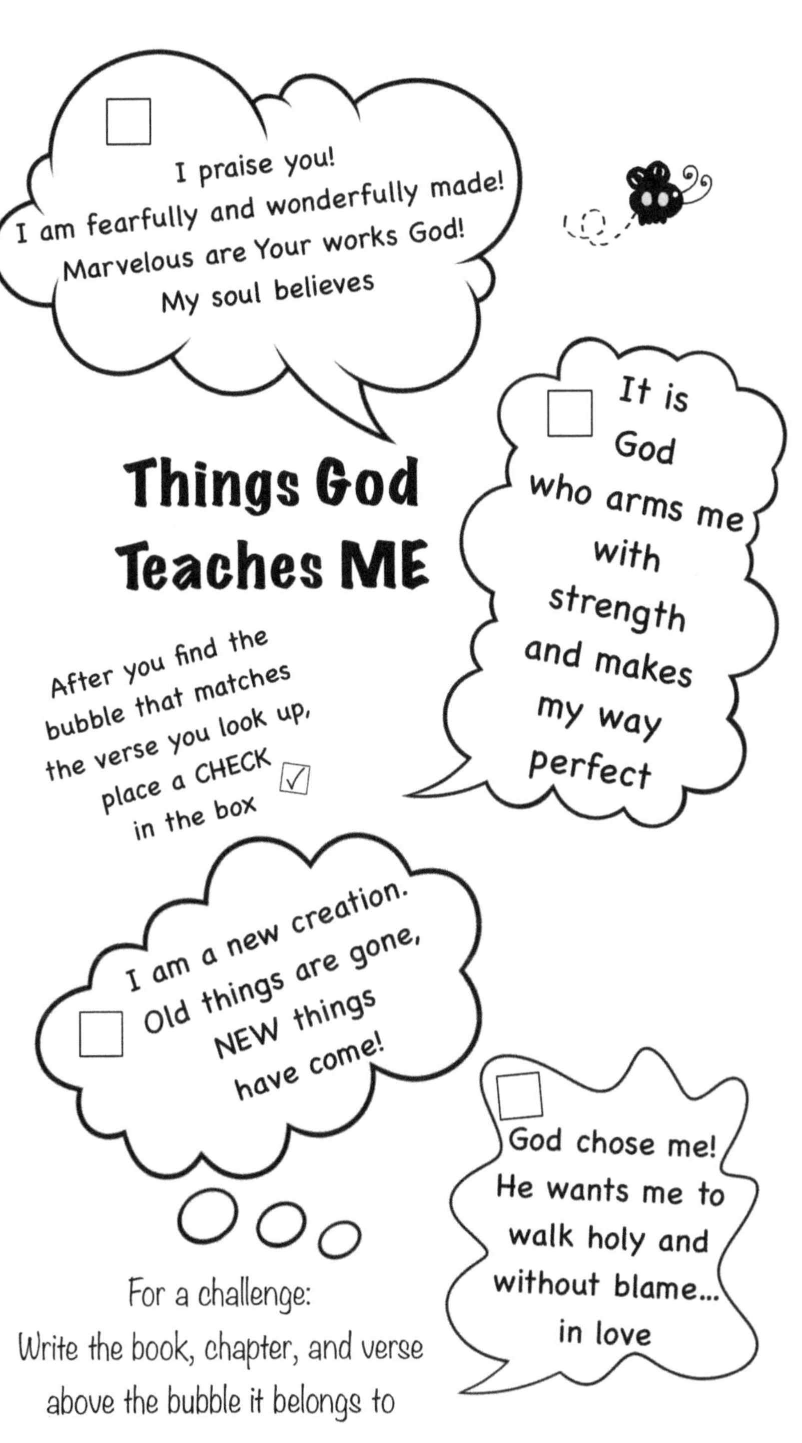

Things God Teaches ME

After you find the bubble that matches the verse you look up, place a CHECK in the box

For a challenge:
Write the book, chapter, and verse above the bubble it belongs to

Meditation

Recently I heard someone say,
"Meditation is becoming one with the Universe."
Hmmmm... the Universe is GINORMOUS!
How exactly do I become one with it???

Let's take a deeper look at meditation
and what God says about it

Psalm Chapter 1, verses 1-3 teaches us to Meditate
[think] about God's law [His Word, the Bible]
When we do, we are keeping ourself safe. He also said
that we would be like a tree planted by flowing
streams, we won't wither [dry up], and we will prosper,
[have the things we need].

Relaxing Techniques

Everyone gets anxious, it can be a normal first response.
But staying in a state of anxiety is not healthy.
It's super important to include calming techniques
while we're catching unhealthy thoughts.
Let's practice...

Your first day in a new classroom?
You naturally feel anxious right!?! 

Here are three things you can do to
take control and help you feel calm...

1. Take a deep breath, let it out slow. Deep, slow breaths increase the flow of blood to your brain, helping you to think clearly, and slows down your racing heart!

2. Think thoughts that are healthy (positive)...
"I am an awesome person. I've got this!
I'm a really good friend. It's going to be okay!"

3. Repeat this to yourself, "I am not alone. God is with me wherever I go, and through Him I can do all things!"

Now YOU try!

Write two situations that make you feel super anxious (or nervous).

____

____

Now list things you can do, to decrease anxiety, and increase assurance in your ability to carry on [keep moving forward]

____

____

____

Hey, you should totally MEMORIZE this!
Philippians 4:6-9, is all really good to read,
but try to memorize [verse 8]
the "think on these things" part!
Well, that's what I call it!
When I'm feeling nervous, scared, or anxiety is
trying to take over, I remind myself to not only
catch unhealthy thoughts, but to also
THINK ON POSITIVE ONES!

"Whatever things are true, whatever things
are honorable, whatever things are just [fair],
whatever things are pure, whatever things are
lovely [acceptable], whatever things are of
GOOD REPORT; if there is any virtue
[excellence], and if there is any praise,
THINK ON THESE THINGS!

Philippians 4:8

So basically, God is telling us to take control
of the thoughts that create anxiety, and instead,
think on things that BRING PEACE!

Okay, your turn
to DRAW!

In this space draw something that belongs
in a fenced area... like maybe your dog,
or a horse that's in training,
or maybe a playground for small children.
It could even be a farmer's cows!

Challenge:
Also, draw a fence with a gate

Does your family have a fence around the yard?
Or maybe your school's outside area?
I bet you've seen a fence around a baseball field.
Why do you think people put up fences in these areas?
Hey, great job! You're right! It's for SAFETY.

GATES

Do you know how to enter a fenced-in area? Of course,
it's called a gate. Gates are entrances for fenced-in areas.

Okay, now let's think about our "mind and heart" as
needing a fence. These areas are SUPER important!
We've learned that reading our Bible is like washing...
keeping our heart and mind clean. We should also protect
(or guard) these areas with a "spiritual fence".
And guess what?
You have GATES, where things can enter.

Okay, your turn!

(Circle) the items that are SAFE
and would be okay to enter your mind and heart.
Then on each line, write which gate (Eyes, Ears, or Both)
where these can enter.

Music with inappropriate words
____

Movies that feel safe, and encouraging
____

Movies that have inappropriate words
____

Conversations that hurt people
____

Conversations that are encouraging
____

Music that feels safe
____

Listening to Worship music
____

Watching shows that create fear
____

Choosing shows that are "clean content" Jesus would watch them with me
____

Great work!

Hey GREAT JOB!

It's super important to recognize things that might try to enter one of your gates!

You may be thinking,
"But, some of those things have already entered."
Don't worry, because when you invited Jesus
to come into your heart, He cleaned those areas!
Now, it's your job to protect them!

In this space, write phrases that you can practice saying to people who may influence (or pressure) you to open a gate...

Here's an example:
"I don't feel comfortable watching this. Hey, let's watch something else!"

How do you define a Good Friend?

What are the characteristics you like in a friend?

Characteristic = a quality
(distinctive attribute or feature)
belonging to a person.

[examples: honest, funny, kind...]

List the name & characteristics of two
of your friends

NAME: _______________________
CHARACTERISTICS:
____
____
____
____

NAME: _______________________
CHARACTERISTICS:
____
____
____
____

Let's talk about
FRIENDSHIPS

Guess what! There will always be someone who "doesn't" like you.
And you know what… it's OKAY!
It's because we don't all have the same personalities. We're all different!
What God wants us to do is to be kind, pray for people, and do good.
He will help you build the friendships that are healthy and safe for you.

Read Luke, Chapter 6, verse 31
[Luke 6:31]

Jesus taught us to treat people the same way we want them to treat us!

Friendship

Forgiving
one
another

Isn't afraid
to be silly

Making
memories
together

Being

Kind

Being

Patient

Being

YOU!

Makes

You

Smile!

Remember, it's okay to choose
your friends carefully.
Your friends should always be people who
"bring out the best in you".
Friends encourage and support
each other!
They are "like-minded"...
they have the same interests and beliefs.

"make my JOY, full, by being like-minded,
having the same love, being of one accord,
of one mind" -Paul
Philippians 2:2

Using the verses on the next page, Write the correct LETTER (A, B, C, or D) on the line, matching them to the correct Book & Chapter
Philippians 4:13
John 14:6
2 Timothy 1:7
Ephesians 2:8

A:
For God did not give us a
spirit of fear, but of power,
and love, and a sound mind

B:
I can do all things
through Christ
who strengthens me!

C:
I am the way, the truth, and the life.
No one comes to the Father
except through me.
-Jesus

D:
By grace you have been
saved through faith, and that
not of yourselves, it is the
gift of God!

**Use these four verses
to match the bubbles
on the previous page...**

Ready for a Science Experiment?

> You will need:
> One Clear Glass measuring cup
> One egg
> 1/3 cup of Salt

- ☐ First, fill the glass measuring cup with 3/4 cold water.

- ☐ Second, place the egg GENTLY into the water.

- ☐ Observation: Did the egg SINK or FLOAT?

- ☐ Next, remove the egg.

- ☐ Now, pour the salt into the water, and stir for 1 minute.

- ☐ Place the egg into the "salted" water.

- ☐ Observation Two:
  Did the egg SINK or FLOAT?

Salt creates DENSITY!
And can help things FLOAT!

A body of water that is SALTY enough to help people float is the "Dead Sea".

The United States also has a salted lake you can float in. It's located in the Western United States It's the "Great Salt Lake" in Utah.

Fun Fact:
The Dead Sea is actually a LAKE! It's located between Israel and Jordan

Guess what!
The Bible talks about SALT too!

Take a moment to look up these verses...

Matthew 5:13-16

&

Colossians 4:6

On the next page, share what you've learned!

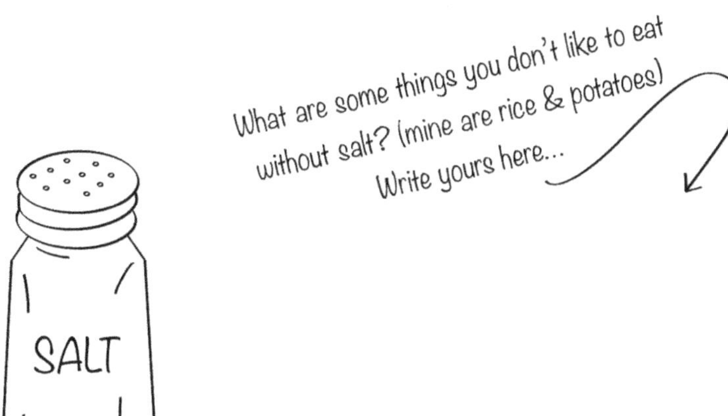

What I learned from Matthew 5:13-16

____

____

____

____

What I learned from Colossians 4:6

____

____

____

____

You did it!
Great work!

I'm so proud of you for thinking about these two scriptures.
Look how much you're
GROWING on the INSIDE!

Think for a second about how the "salted water" helped the egg stay afloat and not sink.
Now imagine for a moment, that you are in a really dark forest, but in the distance you can see a BRIGHT city on a hill! Would you be drawn to that city? Yes! Because no one wants to wander around in a dark forest, ALONE!

God is light! He gives HOPE, so to people who are struggling... we're a LIGHT!
Then when we share God, and the truth we've learned in the Bible, we're SALT!
We help ourselves and others STAY AFLOAT and not sink when there's problems!
Remember, a little salt
can even help things taste better!

Draw YOUR space!
You can draw your home, your school,
your community or even your state!
The space where YOU Shine Bright every day!

You, are a City on a hill for those who feel lost.

Challenge:
Create a MAP of one of your places

? ? Question: ? ?

Does the moon have its own light?

Guess what? The answer is "No"

The moon receives its light

from the sun.

Try this...

You will need:

One flashlight

One small round object

(an orange, an apple, or a small ball)

and a mirror

In one hand hold the flashlight, in your other hand hold the small round object. Shine the flashlight towards the mirror, until it's reflection shines on the round object that's in your hand.

That's kinda Cool, huh!

Moon Phases

Have you ever used Oreo cookies to create the different phases of the moon? If you haven't, you should try it! It's a LOT of fun!

The moon is a ROCK, and the only way it shines is by "reflecting the sun". And guess what! That's exactly what we do... except our sun is spelled "SON". The Son of God, Jesus, shines through us! When we are in tough situations, we can become "dark" in our thinking, OR we can REFLECT THE SON by choosing the Fruit of The Spirit... AND by following the instructions we've learned in the Bible. Remember Colossians 3:12, we "wear it" for others to see!

That's how WE SHINE BRIGHT!

Using a yellow crayon, or colored pencil, fill in the circles to show the different Phases of the Moon

New Moon   Waxing Crescent   First Quarter   Waxing Gibbous

Full Moon   Waning Gibbous   Last Quarter   Waning Crescent

John 15:16

You did not choose me,
but I chose you,
and appointed you, that you
should go and bear FRUIT,
and that your FRUIT
should remain; that whatever
you will ask of the Father
in my name,
He may give it to you.
-Jesus

Guess what?
You've just completed your

Growth

Mindset Journal

You have learned SO MUCH!

You now understand the importance of choosing Healthy thoughts, the importance of reading your Bible, and how to find scripture. You've learned how to use a few calming techniques, and to meditate on God's Word. You also learned how to protect your Gates! You've learned it's okay to choose your friends carefully, and how to be a good friend. You've learned that God wants you to SHINE BRIGHT!

And the most important thing, is that you invited Jesus to live in your heart!

Wow! That is so AWESOME!

Hang on… there's more…

My reflection

To "reflect" is taking the time, unhurried, to consider what you've experienced and learned.

Take a moment to reflect on your Growth Mindset Journal.

- How have you changed?
- How can you continue practicing what you've learned?

____

You are NOT ALONE!

God doesn't want us to walk alone. You've learned that He is with you, wherever you go. And He also wants us to CONNECT with other people who love Him too. If you and your family have a church that you are a part of, GREAT! If you don't, ask your parents (guardians) if they will help you find a church to connect with. Remember, it's important to GROW on the inside. We do that by reading the Bible, by praying and talking with God, and connecting with "like-minded" people who love Him too! I'm so excited for you!
You are SHINING BRIGHT!

You did it!

You've completed the activities in your journal!

My family and I are incredibly proud of you!
Living your life with GOD IN IT,
is the best decision you will ever make!

God loves you!

And He thinks YOU are amazing!

We want to hear from you!
Your parent/guardian can send us a REVIEW to let
us know your thoughts about YOUR JOURNEY
with your Life with Bee Growth Mindset Journal

You and your family can connect with us by using either of these two web addresses...

www.kainonlandmedia.com

www.jenalowry.com

Hey, don't forget to check out our book series,
Life with Bee!

Book One, The Crazy Cool Glove, is available on Amazon
Book Two, The Lost Shoes, will release Fall of 2023

CUT this page out
and hang it somewhere, so you can see it and read it EVERY DAY!

Bee YOURSELF!

Keep Trying!

Everyone makes mistakes

God created ME!

I am Loved!

God SMILES at me!

I Am Valuable!

I am WONDERFULLY made!

www.ingramcontent.com/pod-product-compliance
Lightning Source LLC
Chambersburg PA
CBHW041650150726
48005CB00013BA/1605